P9-CDB-775

There are secrets to success in business, as well as in life. Richard Rybolt learned them as he went, literally, from rags to riches—from selling eggs door-to-door at age thirteen to being a self-made millionaire. One Christmas he decided to compile for his two children the observations, hard lessons, and insider's tips that helped him create a booming business empire. This very special book of timeless business wisdom is the inspiring, eye-opening result.

RICHARD RYBOLT is a real estate developer and the owner and CEO of a large tree nursery. He also holds interests in agriculture, food manufacturing, and retailing. An Ohio native, he now resides in Newfane, New York.

Richard Rybolt

NO CHAIRS MAKE FOR SHORT MEETINGS

And Other Business Maxims from Dad

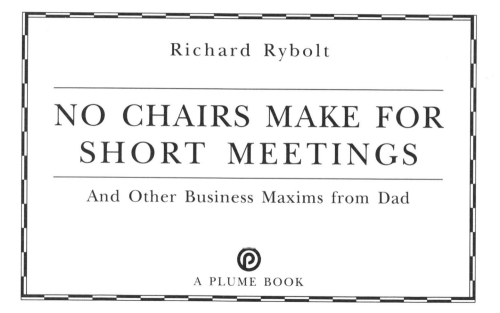

A PLUME BOOK

PLUME • Published by the Penguin Group • Penguin Books USA Inc., 375 Hudson Street, New York, New York 10014, U.S.A. • Penguin Books Ltd, 27 Wrights Lane, London W8 5TZ, England • Penguin Books Australia Ltd, Ringwood, Victoria, Australia • Penguin Books Canada Ltd, 10 Alcorn Avenue, Toronto, Ontario, Canada M4V 3B2 • Penguin Books (N.Z.) Ltd, 182-190 Wairau Road, Auckland 10, New Zealand • Penguin Books Ltd, Registered Offices: Harmondsworth, Middlesex, England • First published by Plume, an imprint of Dutton Signet, a division of Penguin Books USA Inc. • First Printing, June, 1994 • 10 9 8 7 6 5 4 3 • Copyright © Richard E. Rybolt, 1994 • All rights reserved • ℗ REGISTERED TRADEMARK—MARCA REGISTRADA • LIBRARY OF CONGRESS CATALOGING-IN-PUBLICATION DATA: Rybolt, Richard. No chairs make for short meetings : and other business maxims from dad / Richard Rybolt. p. cm. ISBN 0-27194-0 1. Business—Quotations, maxims, etc. I. Title. PN6084.B87R93 1994 650—dc20 94-1908 CIP • Printed in the United States of America • Set in New Baskerville • Designed by Steven N. Stathakis •
• Books are available at quantity discounts when used to promote products or services. For information please write to Premium Marketing Division, Penguin Books USA Inc., 375 Hudson Street, New York, New York 10014.

Dedicated to my mother, who taught me a simple truth:
"I can do anything—if I believe I can."

The principles in this little book of business maxims have been collected, revised, and tested over my lifetime. I offer them to you, my children and grandchildren, in the hope they might spare you the agony of uncovering every truth for yourself. Yet, in reality, I know there is no other way.

Real success comes from breaking rules as well as keeping rules. Ultimately, there is only one definition of success that counts anyway; it is the one you write yourself, for your own life. I pray you will not let anyone else write it for you.

—Dad

ACKNOWLEDGMENTS

To my wife, Anita, who typed and corrected my material, offered helpful suggestions, and encouraged me to keep going amid many distractions.

To my children, Jeffrey and Nancy, whose love has inspired me to tackle this project.

To God, who has allowed me the chance to experience the ultimate adventure—life.

To my agent, Joseph Ajlouny, who built the bridge to my writing success.

The biggest challenge you will have will not be finding a way to correct a problem. The real challenge is seeing the problem in the first place.

THERE WILL BE DAYS WHEN THE ROOF CAVES IN. PROP IT UP AND KEEP ON GO-ING.

A successful business is usually built on many small improvements over time. But, occasionally, there will be rare opportunities to leap ahead. Take that leap while the window is open.

When everyone seems to be headed in the same direction—it may be time to look the other way!

Use profanity to make your point only if you lack the facts.

WHEN THE GUY SAYS, "IT'S NOW OR NEVER," ALWAYS CHOOSE "NEVER."

———

PROBLEM IS SPELLED O-P-P-O-R-T-U-N-I-T-Y.

A CHECK IN THE MAIL IS NOT MONEY IN THE BANK. DO NOT BE TEMPTED TO SPEND IT UNTIL YOU GET IT.

People love applause—offer it generously. Don't wait for a perfect performance.

What worked so well yesterday may be a bust today.

LEARN FROM EVERYONE. EVEN THE JANI-
TOR MAY KNOW MORE THAN YOU WOULD
EVER BELIEVE.

———

LOOK FOR GOOD EVERYWHERE; TROUBLE
WILL SHOW UP ON ITS OWN.

Always give other people the credit for anything good that happens. Credit is like love—the more you give away, the more you have left for yourself.

IF YOU WANT TO HAVE A SHORT MEET-
ING, DON'T PROVIDE CHAIRS.

Believe in "good luck." But also believe it happens most often to people who work hard and keep their eyes open.

ALWAYS TRY TO DELIVER A LITTLE MORE
THAN YOU PROMISED.

———

NOT MANY CRISES ARE AS BAD AS THEY
FIRST SEEM.

When you stop worrying about who gets the credit—*you* do!

———

Love what you do (most of the time) or find a different job.

YOUR WORST DECISION WILL BE THE ONE
YOU NEVER MADE.

———

NO MATTER WHAT—NEVER COMPROMISE
WHAT YOU BELIEVE IN.

There are two good reasons to promote your own people: 1. Outsiders are rarely as good as they first seem. 2. Promotion from within gives hope to everyone else there.

Make no decisions when you're angry.

———

Be courageous enough to stand up and speak out for what you believe—especially when everyone else disagrees.

HEALTH OR WEALTH? IT'S SUCH AN OBVI-OUS CHOICE THAT YOU WONDER WHY SO MANY PEOPLE CHOOSE THE WRONG ONE.

Courage is sticking your neck out for something you believe in. It's an action, not a thought.

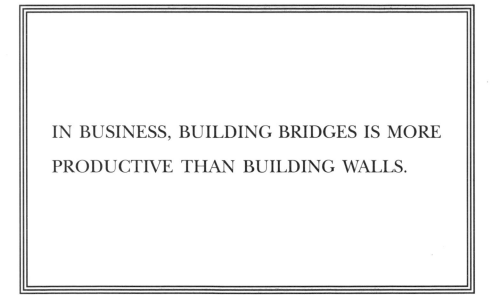

IN BUSINESS, BUILDING BRIDGES IS MORE
PRODUCTIVE THAN BUILDING WALLS.

YOU NEED TO CHANGE ONLY ONE THING
TO TURN AN AVERAGE PERSON INTO A
GREAT SUCCESS—THEIR ATTITUDE. BUT
BEWARE, IT'S THE TOUGHEST JOB OF ALL.

If it ain't broke—better start fixing it anyway.

———

If you really want to hurt your critics, act like you never heard their criticism.

BE KIND TO MY KIDS AND YOU HAVE A
SUCKER IN YOUR GRASP.

Make it crystal clear that everyone works for the same person—the customer. Without satisfying the customer, no one works at all.

Many people knock wealth—but few people choose poverty.

Business is a game—maybe an important game—but still a game. Don't get too serious about it.

TRY TO FIND SOMETHING LIKABLE ABOUT EVERYONE. IF YOU CAN'T, AT LEAST UNDERSTAND WHERE THEY ARE COMING FROM.

The highest wage always goes to people who can motivate others to achieve success. You can never achieve success alone.

PROMISES KEPT ARE WHAT SUCCESSFUL
BUSINESSES ARE BUILT ON.

Action—not reaction. The words sound similar, but the result is totally different.

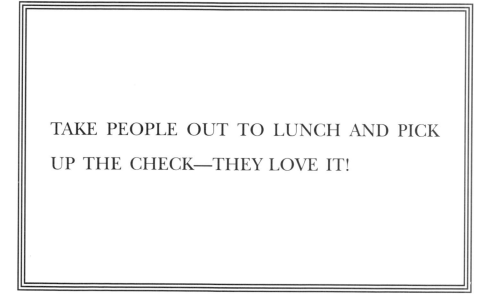

TAKE PEOPLE OUT TO LUNCH AND PICK
UP THE CHECK—THEY LOVE IT!

It is always best to have all the information before you make a decision. However, there will be times when you just can't wait any longer. Use your best judgment and move on.

Keep a *Things to Do* list and revise it every day.

———

The worst feeling is walking away from a meeting knowing you had something to say—but didn't.

One outstanding person is usually worth at least three mediocre ones.

———

Be willing to try almost anything once— or better yet twice!

NEVER INTERRUPT AN IMPORTANT TASK OR MEETING BY ANSWERING A PHONE CALL (UNLESS IT IS FROM YOUR BOSS OR YOUR SPOUSE!).

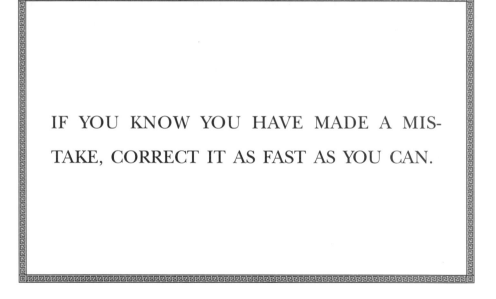

IF YOU KNOW YOU HAVE MADE A MIS-
TAKE, CORRECT IT AS FAST AS YOU CAN.

Showing your anger occasionally is okay—it makes you human. There may even be times you should feign anger to get your point across. But never let anger cause you to lose control of yourself or the situation.

"WE TRIED THAT BEFORE" IS THE RIGHT ANSWER IF YOU WANT TO KILL INITIATIVE.

———

BE DECISIVE—FENCE RIDERS NEVER WIN BIG.

Show *all* of your people the "big picture" if you want the best performance.

———

Forget tricks, deception, and hocus-pocus—unless you're in the magic business.

Take chances. Assume risk. But try to keep the odds in your favor. Risk is what business is all about.

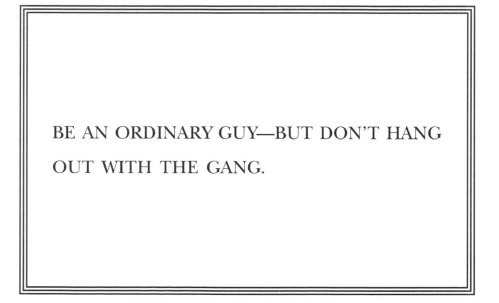

BE AN ORDINARY GUY—BUT DON'T HANG
OUT WITH THE GANG.

You may think titles for menial jobs are unimportant. But who wants to be a garbage collector when they could be a sanitation engineer?

NEVER BE AFRAID TO SAY, "I WAS WRONG."

———

PERCEPTION *IS* REALITY—AS FAR AS YOUR
CUSTOMER IS CONCERNED.

The sooner you realize how short life is, the quicker you will write your own agenda.

IF THE PEOPLE WHO WORK FOR YOU
FEAR YOU, DON'T TRUST ANYTHING THEY
SAY.

There will be a time when loud-mouthed, incompetent people seem to be getting the best of you. When that happens, you only have to be patient and wait for them to self-destruct. It never fails!

You should never be so far up that you have to look down on anyone.

———

"Tough but fair" is an excellent business reputation to have.

Doubt will try to seep into every crack. Plug those cracks with optimism.

Disagree without being disagreeable. It is an art worth practicing.

ALWAYS KEEP A *TICKLER FILE* TO REMIND YOU TO RECONSIDER SOMETHING AT AN APPROPRIATE FUTURE DATE.

A sure sign of success is when, after years of hard work, worry, and struggle, you hear someone say, "Everything he touches turns to gold."

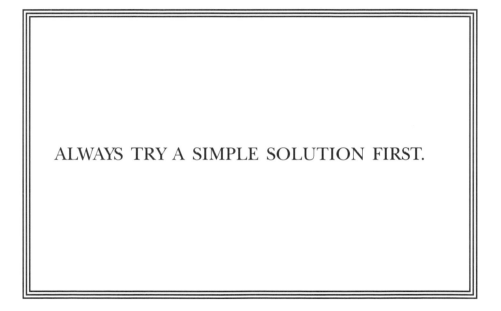

ALWAYS TRY A SIMPLE SOLUTION FIRST.

Some things that sound too good to be true really *are* true; keep your eyes open for them and move fast!

WHENEVER POSSIBLE, ELIMINATE EVERY RULE, REGULATION, AND POLICY AND RE-PLACE THEM WITH FOUR WORDS: "GET THE JOB DONE."

ALWAYS FOCUS ON WHAT IS RIGHT—NOT WHO IS RIGHT.

———

LOOK AT YOUR MAIL ONE TIME. ACT ON IT—OR THROW IT AWAY.

A small business can judge the worth of an employee by the number of customers who ask if the employee is the owner.

Take the biggest risks while you're young—and be a little more conservative as you get older.

NEVER COUNT ON GOOD LUCK—BUT AC-
CEPT IT WITH GRATITUDE.

"JUST DO IT!" IS A MOTTO WORTH
ADOPTING.

IF THERE IS SOMETHING YOU ARE SURE YOU DON'T WANT TO DO, SAY SO WITHOUT FLINCHING—BUT HAVE YOUR REASONS READY.

Praise! Praise! Praise! Nothing will pay higher dividends.

People who know all the answers usually don't understand the questions.

Sometimes you will succeed. Sometimes you will fail. But remember—both provide valuable experience you can bank for the future.

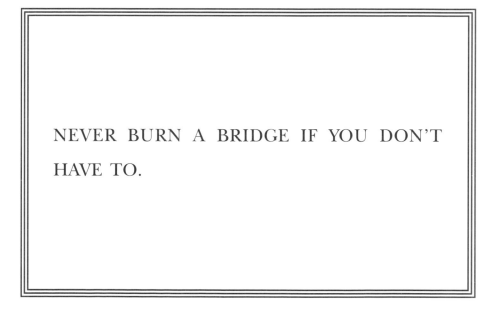

NEVER BURN A BRIDGE IF YOU DON'T HAVE TO.

Never belittle someone or try to make them look bad—especially in front of others. Sooner or later they will get you back.

Numbers will sometimes point you to a conclusion that is totally wrong. You always need more than the numbers.

THE BEST JOB SECURITY IS TO BE WORTH
MORE THAN YOU ARE PAID.

When you find that person with extraordinary talent and ambition, clear the path and pay the price—they are worth it!

BUSINESS SUCCESS IS GRATIFYING, BUT THE MEMORIES YOU WILL SAVOR MOST ARE THOSE OF TIMES YOU SPEND WITH YOUR FAMILY.

Creativity is not restricted to art. Use your mind to see new, untried ways to improve everything you do.

———

If you want to really flatter someone, ask for their help.

When you don't know, say you don't know. But you should never have to say it twice.

HELPING PEOPLE SOLVE PROBLEMS IS A
SURER WAY TO WEALTH THAN TRYING TO
MAKE MONEY.

If a problem or misunderstanding develops between you and someone else, give it a day to cool off, then go to that person and straighten it out.

When you answer the phone and someone you have never heard of is calling you by your first name—beware.

———

The truth is that nice guys usually finish first.

BLUFFING IS LIKE WALKING THE HIGH
WIRE WITHOUT A SAFETY NET TO CATCH
YOU.

Make all job descriptions only one sentence long and exactly the same for everyone: "You are to do whatever it takes to get your work done and make this company successful."

PERFECTION IS AN IMPERFECT GOAL.

———

ORGANIZATION CHARTS ARE LIKE A MAZE
LEADING NOWHERE—SKIP THEM ALTO-
GETHER.

Every morning brings a new day. So forget the shortcomings of yesterday and start over knowing you have another chance to succeed—365 times every year!

WORK! WORK! WORK! SORRY TO HAVE TO TELL YOU, BUT IT'S THE ONLY ROUTE I KNOW TO SUCCESS.

Remember, there is a better way to do everything—so keep looking.

———

Nothing ever costs less than you first thought, but a lot of things will cost more.

IF YOU WANT PEOPLE TO WORK HARDER
AND ACHIEVE MORE, GIVE THEM A VOICE
IN SETTING THEIR OWN GOALS.

You may think you don't have the time to do it right, but you will always find the time to do it over.

———

Pick your battles carefully—you cannot fight them all!

IF YOU TRY A NEW IDEA AND IT FAILS,
KEEP TINKERING WITH IT AND TRY AGAIN.
YOU MAY BE ONLY AN INCH AWAY FROM
REAL SUCCESS.

If the choice is between opportunity and security—choose opportunity.

Most truly great ideas sound preposterous at first.

Watch out for employees who have perfected the art of looking busy but actually accomplish very little.

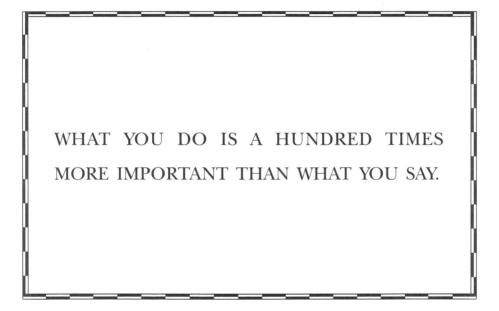

WHAT YOU DO IS A HUNDRED TIMES
MORE IMPORTANT THAN WHAT YOU SAY.

PAY YOUR BILLS QUICKLY—AND WATCH
HOW FAST AND HOW FAR A SUPPLIER
WILL BEND TO KEEP YOUR BUSINESS.

The best way to get people to believe in you is to believe in yourself.

———

There will be days you will need to pretend you have energy and optimism, but soon pretending becomes reality.

Make other people feel important and soon *you* will be important.

Understand that you are both a teacher and a pupil: As you teach you learn; as you learn you teach.

FIND A JOB YOU REALLY LOVE AND YOU WILL NEVER WORK ANOTHER DAY IN YOUR LIFE.

PAY ATTENTION TO YOUR COMPETITORS—
BUT CONCENTRATE 99 PERCENT OF YOUR
ATTENTION ON YOUR OWN BUSINESS.

Good and bad often masquerade as each other. Don't be fooled.

———

Know what you're aiming for—a fuzzy target is hard to hit.

Looking back occasionally at the past will help you chart the best course for the future.

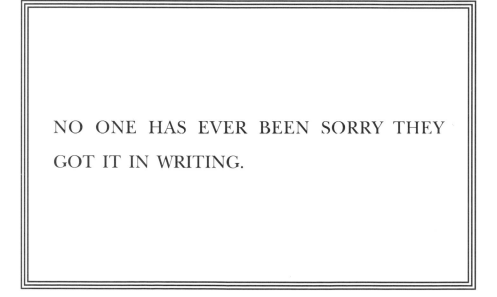

NO ONE HAS EVER BEEN SORRY THEY GOT IT IN WRITING.

JOT DOWN IDEAS AND RIP OUT ARTICLES
AS YOU READ OR YOU WILL NEVER FIND
THEM AGAIN.

Passion is exhilarating in love and in business, but let it cool a little before you make a commitment.

SPEED UP EVERYTHING! FAST IS MORE EX-
CITING AND MORE EFFECTIVE. SLOW IS
DRUDGERY—PEOPLE HATE IT.

Avoid negative people like the plague!

———

To paraphrase Lincoln, "It's not so much where you are that's important—it's the direction that you're tending to go!"

GO IN EARLY IF NECESSARY. STAY LATE IF
NECESSARY. BUT TRAIN YOURSELF NOT
TO BRING YOUR JOB HOME WITH YOU.

Fear of failure: It causes more failure than anything else.

You can buy a person's time and talent—but loyalty and enthusiasm you must earn.

Check the trash cans and the scrap bins. You will be surprised at how much of your profit gets thrown away.

———

Never take a partner solely because you need their money.

FOCUS YOUR EFFORT ON A FEW THINGS THAT WILL MAKE A MAJOR DIFFERENCE. TRY TO DO EVERYTHING AND YOU DO NOTHING.

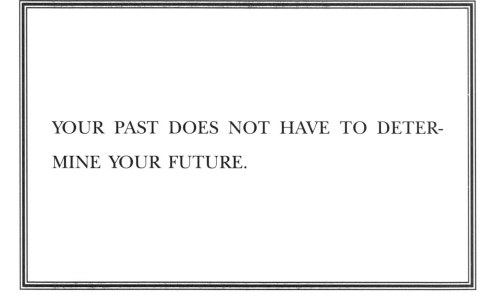

YOUR PAST DOES NOT HAVE TO DETER-
MINE YOUR FUTURE.

Taking yourself too seriously is a mistake. A hundred years from now no one will even remember your name.

Be patient toward people—but impatient about their mistakes.

———

You will get about what you expect—so expect a lot!

SOLICIT ADVICE FROM ALMOST EVERY-
ONE. PEOPLE LOVE TO BE ASKED THEIR
OPINION, AND EVERY NOW AND THEN A
GREAT IDEA WILL SURFACE.

Each customer is like a tree that branches out everywhere—you never lose just *one* customer.

————

If you swim with the sharks, expect the water to turn red.

STAND UP FOR YOUR PEOPLE, LOOK OUT FOR YOUR PEOPLE, CARE ABOUT YOUR PEOPLE—AND THEY WILL CARE ABOUT YOU.

When you have to let someone go, be swift but gentle. Let them down as easy as you can and offer them hope. But get it done now and get on with business.

Change! Change! Change! But never for change's sake.

———

There are times when the best thing you can do is walk away and come back another day.

EVERYTHING IN LIFE REQUIRES A PRICE.
KNOW HOW MUCH YOU'RE WILLING TO
PAY.

A business that provides few opportunities will have trouble keeping outstanding people.

Wait for a perfect time to launch a new product or a new business and you will wait forever.

How you dress has nothing to do with your ability to succeed. However, it may affect your success.

When they promise you, "You can't lose,"
tell them to get lost.

———

In a new position of responsibility, make
a couple of bold moves fast.

THE REAL CHALLENGE OF A GOOD MANAGER IS NOT TO FIND SUPERIOR PEOPLE BUT TO MOTIVATE ORDINARY PEOPLE TO DO SUPERIOR WORK.

Rid your business of complaining crybabies and troublemakers immediately—even if they are talented and hardworking.

———

Today's success erases yesterday's failures.

SET SPECIFIC GOALS AND MAKE THEM
YOUR YARDSTICK TO MEASURE PROG-
RESS.

———

IF YOU *THINK* YOU CAN'T, YOU CAN'T!

If you have put off doing something because you don't know where to start, pick a time and start anywhere.

———

If you have nothing to say—say nothing.

Bad stuff often comes in bunches. There is no rationale for this, except that it's true.

———————

Better figure out what business you are really in, or you will soon be out of business.

INSIST ON FOLLOWING TRADITION IN BUSINESS AND YOU'RE LIKELY TO BE HISTORY.

Small things—a thank you, a note of appreciation, an act of kindness—can pay big dividends.

THE MEMORY OF FAILURE MAKES SUC-
CESS SO MUCH SWEETER!

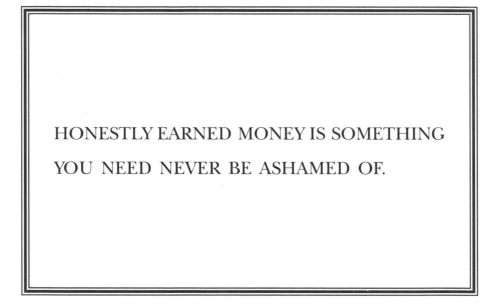

HONESTLY EARNED MONEY IS SOMETHING
YOU NEED NEVER BE ASHAMED OF.